Unraveling the Chains Of Poverty

Understanding the Why

OS ANUMA

Table of Contents

3. Historical Perspectives on Poverty

- Poverty Through the Ages

- Societal Structures and Poverty

- Lessons from Histo

4. The Economic Factors

- Income Disparities

- Wealth Inequality

- Employment Challenges

- The Role of Education

- Impact of Technological Advancements

5. Social Factors

- Discrimination and Marginalization

- Family Structure

- Access to Healthcare

- Social Safety Nets

6. Psychological Factors

- Self-Esteem and Confidence

- Learned Helplessness

- Mental Health and Poverty

- The Poverty Mindset

7. Political Factors

- Government Policies and Poverty

- Corruption and Poverty

- Political Instability

- Global Economic Systems

8. Environmental Factors

- Climate Change and Poverty

- Natural Disasters

- Resource Scarcity

- Environmental Justice

CHAPTER 1:

Introduction

The Enigma of Poverty

The topic of poverty is a haunting enigma that has persisted throughout human history. It transcends borders, cultures, and continents, affecting millions of lives in its relentless grasp. While poverty may manifest differently across the globe, its underlying causes remain constant, and understanding these causes is the first step toward addressing this profound issue.

Purpose and Scope of the Book

This book aims to delve deep into the various facets of poverty, exploring the intricate web of factors that contribute to it. By the end of this journey, readers will have a comprehensive understanding of why poverty persists in our world today. It is our hope that this knowledge will inspire action and drive positive change.

CHAPTER 2:

Defining Poverty

Absolute vs. Relative Poverty

Before we dissect the reasons behind poverty, we must first establish a clear definition of what poverty entails. Poverty can be categorized into two main types: absolute and relative.

Absolute poverty is the condition in which an individual or family lacks the resources to meet their basic human needs, such as food, clean water, shelter, and clothing. This definition provides a universal benchmark, irrespective of a particular society's economic standing.

Relative poverty, on the other hand, is a more complex concept. It refers to the condition where individuals or families have significantly fewer resources and opportunities compared to the majority of people in their society. It takes into account the relative disparities in income, education, and overall quality of life within a particular community or country.

The Multidimensional Nature of Poverty

Poverty is not limited to economic factors alone. It is a multidimensional issue that encompasses various aspects of life, including social, psychological, political, and environmental factors. Understanding this multidimensionality is crucial in unravelling the why behind poverty.

Global Poverty Statistics

To grasp the gravity of the issue, let's examine some global poverty statistics:

As of 2018, the number of people, of the world's population, lived in extreme poverty (living on less than $1.90 per day), according to the World Bank. In 2016, the global income distribution showed that the top 50% of the world's population owned over 46% of the world's wealth, highlighting the staggering wealth inequality.

According to world health organization, 5.2 million children under the age of 5 years die each day due to poverty-related causes, such as lack of access to clean water, nutrition, and healthcare.

These statistics serve as a sobering reminder of the magnitude of the poverty crisis and the urgency of addressing it comprehensively.

CHAPTER 3:

Historical Perspectives On Poverty

Poverty through the Ages

To understand the contemporary factors contributing to poverty, it's essential to take a historical perspective. Poverty has been a constant companion of humanity, evolving alongside societal structures and economic systems.

In ancient civilizations, poverty was often attributed to factors like famine, war, and natural disasters. As societies progressed, poverty became increasingly linked to economic disparities and the distribution of resources.

Societal Structures and Poverty

Throughout history, societal structures have played a pivotal role in perpetuating or alleviating poverty. Feudal systems, for example, concentrated wealth and power among the nobility, while peasants lived in abject poverty. Similarly, colonialism led to the exploitation and impoverishment of indigenous populations in various parts of the world.

Lessons from History

History provides valuable lessons on the causes of poverty and how societies have tackled this issue. For instance, the Industrial Revolution, while contributing to economic growth, also gave rise to exploitative labour practices and increased income inequality. However, it also sparked social movements that eventually led to labour reforms and improvements in living conditions for the working class.

Understanding the historical context of poverty can shed light on how economic, social, and political factors have intertwined to shape the modern landscape of poverty.

CHAPTER 4:

The Economic Factors

Income Disparities

Income disparities are at the heart of the poverty issue. When a significant portion of a population earns substantially less than others, poverty becomes inevitable. Several key economic factors contribute to income disparities:

Wage Inequality: The gap between the wages of high-income earners and low-income workers has been widening over the years. Factors such as automation, globalization, and shifts in the job market have exacerbated this gap.

Unemployment and Underemployment: Lack of access to stable employment opportunities or underemployment (where individuals work part-time or in low-wage jobs) can push people into poverty.

Economic Recessions: Economic downturns can lead to job losses, reduced income, and increased poverty rates, affecting vulnerable populations the most.

Wealth Inequality

Wealth inequality refers to the unequal distribution of assets and resources among individuals and households. While income inequality focuses on the flow of money, wealth inequality considers the accumulation of assets over time. Key factors contributing to wealth inequality include:

Inheritance and Family Wealth: Wealth often passes from one generation to another, reinforcing disparities. Those born into wealthy families have greater access to resources, education, and opportunities.

Investment Income: People with substantial investments in stocks, real estate, or businesses can generate income without actively working, further increasing their wealth.

Tax Policies: Favourable tax policies for the wealthy can allow them to accumulate wealth at a faster rate, widening the wealth gap.

Employment Challenges

Access to stable and well-paying employment is a critical factor in poverty alleviation. However, several challenges hinder job creation and access to employment:

Structural Unemployment: Changes in industries and

technology can result in structural unemployment, where people lack the skills needed for available jobs.

Informal Labour Markets: Many individuals work in the informal sector, which often lacks job security, benefits, and legal protections.

Gender Disparities: Gender-based discrimination in the job market can limit economic opportunities for women.

The Role of Education

Education is both a determinant and a potential solution

to poverty. Access to quality education can break the cycle of poverty by providing individuals with the skills and knowledge needed to secure better-paying jobs. However, educational disparities persist globally, preventing many from realizing their potential.

Impact of Technological Advancements

While technological advancements have brought about numerous benefits, they have also disrupted traditional job markets and exacerbated income disparities. Automation and artificial intelligence are increasingly replacing manual labor, which can lead to job displacement and income inequality.

Understanding these economic factors is crucial in addressing poverty, as they influence both the causes and potential solutions to this complex issue.

CHAPTER 5:

Social Factors

Discrimination and Marginalization

Discrimination and marginalization based on race, gender, ethnicity, religion, or other factors can significantly contribute to poverty. These social factors often result in unequal access to opportunities, resources, and social benefits. Key points to consider include:

Racial and Ethnic Disparities: Minority groups may face systemic discrimination in education, employment, housing, and criminal justice systems, leading to higher poverty rates.

Gender Inequality: Women, on average, earn less than men for the same work and are more likely to experience poverty due to factors such as the gender pay gap and the unequal division of unpaid care work.

Age Discrimination: Older adults and youth may face discrimination in the job market, limiting their employment opportunities and increasing their vulnerability to poverty.

Family Structure

Family structure can influence an individual's likelihood of experiencing poverty. Single-parent households, for instance, often face higher poverty rates due to the challenges of providing for a family on a single income. Understanding the dynamics of family structure and their impact on poverty is essential.

Access to Healthcare

Access to healthcare is a critical social factor influencing poverty. Inadequate access to healthcare can lead to high medical expenses, decreased productivity, and increased poverty. The burden of healthcare costs can be particularly severe in countries without comprehensive healthcare systems.

Social Safety Nets

The presence and effectiveness of social safety nets can mitigate the impact of poverty. These safety nets include programs such as unemployment benefits, food assistance, and housing subsidies. The availability and generosity of such programs vary widely between countries and regions, impacting poverty rates.

Understanding how discrimination, family structure, access to healthcare, and social safety nets intersect with poverty is vital in addressing the social dimensions of this complex issue.

Chapter 6:

Psychological Factors

Self-Esteem and Confidence

Psychological factors can play a significant role in perpetuating poverty. Low self-esteem and lack of confidence can hinder individuals from pursuing opportunities for personal and economic growth. The cycle of poverty often erodes self-worth, making it difficult for individuals to break free from its grip.

Learned Helplessness

Learned helplessness is a psychological concept where individuals come to believe that their actions have no impact on their circumstances. In the context of poverty, it can manifest as a belief that no matter how hard one tries, they cannot escape poverty. This mindset can be a significant barrier to taking proactive steps to improve one's situation.

Mental Health and Poverty

There is a complex relationship between poverty and mental health. Poverty can lead to increased stress, anxiety, and depression, while pre-existing mental health conditions can make it harder for individuals to escape poverty. Access to mental healthcare and support is often limited for those living in poverty.

The Poverty Mindset

The poverty mindset refers to a set of beliefs and attitudes that can trap individuals in a cycle of poverty. Common elements of the poverty mindset include fatalism (believing that one's fate is predetermined), short-term thinking (prioritizing immediate needs over long-term goals), and resistance to change (due to fear or uncertainty).

Understanding these psychological factors is crucial in developing strategies to empower individuals to overcome poverty and build self-sufficiency.

CHAPTER 7:

Political Factors

Government Policies and Poverty

Government policies can either exacerbate or alleviate poverty. Policies related to taxation, social programs, labour laws, and economic regulations all have a direct impact on income distribution and poverty rates. Some policies may favour the wealthy, while others may provide a safety net for the poor.

Corruption and Poverty

Corruption within governments and institutions can divert resources away from poverty alleviation efforts. When funds intended for social programs, infrastructure development, or healthcare are embezzled or mismanaged, the impact on poverty can be devastating.

Political Instability

Political instability, including armed conflict and civil unrest, can lead to economic downturns and displacement of populations. These disruptions can push people into poverty and hinder poverty alleviation efforts.

Global Economic Systems

The global economic system also plays a role in perpetuating poverty. International trade agreements, debt burdens on developing countries, and unequal access to global markets can all contribute to economic disparities between nations.

Understanding the political dimensions of poverty is crucial in advocating for policy changes and systemic reforms that can address the root causes of poverty.

CHAPTER 8:

Environmental Factors

Climate Change and Poverty

Climate change poses a unique threat to poverty reduction efforts. Vulnerable populations, often located in low-income regions, are disproportionately affected by the impacts of climate change, including extreme weather events, crop failures, and displacement.

Natural Disasters

Natural disasters such as hurricanes, earthquakes, and floods can devastate communities and push them into poverty. Vulnerable infrastructure and lack of disaster preparedness exacerbate the impact of these events on impoverished populations.

Resource Scarcity

Resource scarcity, including water and arable land, can

lead to conflict and poverty in resource-dependent regions. Competition for limited resources can result in displacement, food insecurity, and economic instability.

Environmental Justice

Environmental justice is a concept that highlights the unequal distribution of environmental benefits and burdens. Low-income communities often bear the brunt of pollution, hazardous waste, and environmental degradation, leading to adverse health effects and economic challenges.

Understanding the intersection of environmental factors

and poverty is crucial in addressing the impacts of environmental changes on vulnerable populations.

Chapter 9:

Breaking The Chains

Poverty Alleviation Programs

Various poverty alleviation programs and initiatives exist globally to address the multifaceted nature of poverty. These programs may include:

Cash Transfer Programs: Providing direct financial assistance to low-income families to meet basic needs.

Education and Skill Development: Offering training and

education programs to enhance employability and income-earning potential.

Microfinance and Entrepreneurship Support: Facilitating access to small loans and business development support for individuals and communities.

Grassroots Initiatives

Local community efforts play a vital role in poverty alleviation. Grassroots initiatives involve community members identifying their specific needs and collectively working toward solutions. These efforts can range from community gardens to educational programs and job training.

Education and Skill Development

Investing in education and skill development is a powerful strategy for breaking the cycle of poverty. Access to quality education, vocational training, and lifelong learning opportunities can empower individuals to secure better employment and improve their economic prospects.

Empowering Communities

Empowering marginalized communities to participate in decision-making processes, advocate for their rights, and access resources is essential in addressing poverty. Community empowerment can lead to sustainable, locally-driven solutions.

CHAPTER 10:

Conclusion

A Call to Action

The causes of poverty are multifaceted and deeply intertwined, encompassing economic, social, psychological, political, and environmental factors. To address poverty comprehensively, we must recognize that there is no one-size-fits-all solution. Instead, a holistic approach that considers the unique circumstances of each community and individual is required.

The Path to a Poverty-Free World

Eliminating poverty requires concerted efforts at local national and global levels. It necessitates policies that promote economic equity, social justice, and environmental sustainability. It also requires collective action, advocacy, and a commitment to dismantling the systemic barriers that perpetuate poverty.

Final Thoughts

As we conclude our exploration into the "why" behind poverty, we are left with a profound understanding of the complexity of this issue. Poverty is not solely the result of individual choices or circumstances but is deeply embedded in the structures and systems of our societies.

It is our hope that this book has shed light on the multifaceted nature of poverty, inspiring readers to become advocates for change, champions of social justice, and allies in the fight against poverty. Only through collective action and a commitment to justice can we aspire to build a world free from the chains of poverty, where every individual has the opportunity to thrive.

www.ingramcontent.com/pod-product-compliance
Lightning Source LLC
Chambersburg PA
CBHW071010260726

48661CB00007B/2885